How Anna The Elf Saved Christmas!

Lionel Quartus Lowery II

AuthorHouse™
1663 Liberty Drive
Bloomington, IN 47403
www.authorhouse.com
Phone: 833-262-8899

Because of the dynamic nature of the Internet, any web addresses or links contained in this book may have changed
since publication and may no longer be valid. The views expressed in this work are solely those of the author and do
not necessarily reflect the views of the publisher, and the publisher hereby disclaims any responsibility for them.

Any people depicted in stock imagery provided by Getty Images are models,
and such images are being used for illustrative purposes only.
Certain stock imagery © Getty Images.

This book is printed on acid-free paper.

ISBN: 979-8-8230-3625-2 (sc)
       979-8-8230-3623-8 (hc)
       979-8-8230-3624-5 (e)

Library of Congress Control Number: 2024922191

Print information available on the last page.

Published by AuthorHouse 10/18/2024

authorHOUSE

How Anna The ELF Saved Christmas!

One Christmas Eve, with peace in the air

It was ever so cold, with snow everywhere.

A blur in the sky lit up the night.

T'was Santa, his sleigh, and reindeer in flight.

3

Suddenly Santa heard a huge rip.

Then Dasher's old saddle started to slip.

Then Dancer and Prancer shifted with force,

And Vixen and Blitzen were lifted off-course.

Whenever dear Santa had a huge problem

He knew where to go and who always solved them.

The Saddle Factory, was part of his plan

And up on the roof is where he would land.

With a blink of an eye and a shift of his nose,

The landing was delicate, and light as a rose.

Down the chimney he came, quick as a snap.

Brushed dirt off his boot and soot from his hat.

On his way up the stairs, he felt a great tug.

He pulled himself free with the grip of his glove.

11

Anna yelled, "Santa! It's been a whole year.

I missed you so much. I'm glad you are here."

Santa kneeled down and hugged her with might.

He'd missed her so much, and held her so tight.

Santa looked down. "Oh, my button is gone!"

"I'll sew a new one back on. It won't take too long!
Follow me, Santa, I have reins galore.
I'll fix every problem, all that and more.
I'll fix the rein, and mend all the tack,
Sew a button back, and fix every strap!"

15

He gave Anna his jacket,

And inspected the saddles.

As he walked toward he tack,

The floor started to rattle.

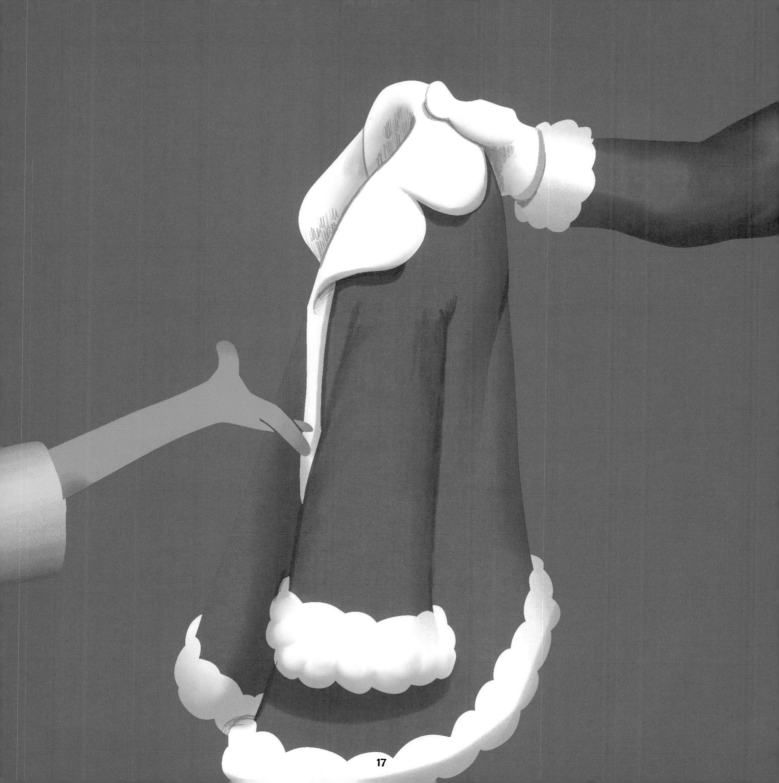

17

She almost forgot. It would have been tragic.

For even one button to be without magic.

She reached in her pouch, Faith gave a bark,

Anna sprinkled that button with that magical spark.

Then Anna hugged Santa, and shouted with glee,
"Load it all up," and watched Santa flee.

Up off the roof, and into the night,
Santa went poof, and flew out of sight.

Anna just smiled and pushed back her hair,

then she saw something there, stuck on the stairs.

Was it a mitten? But surely it wasn't.

But a piece of his jacket, and a big wooden button.

She was going to grab it, Santa might fret.

But she left it right there, so she'd never forget.

The End

About the Author

Lionel Quartus Lowery II is a husband, father, and man of faith. He is also certified as a Medical Laboratory Scientist and served in the United States Army for over 32 years. As a young child who loved science and enjoyed reading about adventures, he joined the Army on a quest to create his own adventures. While in the Military, he lived in many places and traveled all over the world. Over the years, he served in many leadership positions and was entrusted with opportunities to teach, lead, and mentor thousands of people. Often, he used stories to teach Military students and help soldiers and civilian employees understand the Army mission. In doing this, he learned an important lesson. He learned that it wasn't about him, nor was it about his stories. Instead, it was how those stories brought people together. Now, he knows what truly matters- his sincere care for people and what he can do to unite them. This experience enabled him to develop the credible insight required to create the Lowery Care Construct. In this concept, he explains that he cares about people, places, and things- in that order. With irreversible momentum, Lionel is determined to share the same INSPIRE formula that saved his life, inspire others by helping them find their future self, and use stories to bring everyone together.